Contents

Hundreds of marathons are run all over the world. Six are part of the World Marathon Challenge: Tokyo, Berlin, London, New York, Boston, and Chicago (above).

Chapter 1

Marathon Run History

Today, it is fairly common to see **marathon** races on the streets of major cities. But did you know that the marathon is actually one of the oldest sporting competitions on earth? The origins of the marathon come from the legends of the ancient Greeks. According to one of these tales, a messenger named **Pheidippides** ran from the battlefield of Marathon to Athens to bring news that the Greeks had defeated their rivals, the Persians in the Battle of Marathon. Pheidippides is said to have burst out, "Rejoice! We have conquered!" before dying from the exertions of his run.

Today's marathon distance of 26 miles, 385 yards (42.2 km) comes from the 1908 Olympics in London, England. The race had been run at a distance of about 25 miles (40 km), but in London, organizers wanted the race to start at Windsor Castle, before going onto London's streets and ending with a lap of the White City Stadium, with the finishing line in front of the Royal Box. When all that distance was added up, it came to the 26 miles, 385 yards mark – and runners have been using it ever since!

Boston Marathon

The Boston Marathon is the world's most famous road running race. Held on the third Monday of every April – a day known as **Patriots' Day** in the state of Massachusetts, where Boston is located – it is also the world's oldest annual race over the official marathon distance of 26 miles, 385 yards (42.2 km).

The first Boston Marathon took place in 1897, and had less than twenty runners – and only ten finishers. But today, organizers from the Boston Athletic Association (**BAA**) welcome in the range of 25,000-30,000 runners every time the race is held.

Because of the huge popularity of the race, a large percentage of the participants must run qualifying times, based on their age and gender, in other races to gain entry to Boston. The top places are always very hotly contested, with large cash prizes at stake for the fastest men and women. Runners from East Africa – Kenya and Ethiopia – have dominated the race since the early 1990s.

There are also divisions for wheelchair and handcycle athletes. Because of the huge number of runners, participants actually start at different times, known as "waves," in Hopkinton, a small town just outside of Boston.

More Than Just a Race

The Boston Marathon, however, is much more than just a running race. For runners around the world, it represents a classic challenge – something to train and strive for, as proof that you truly are a "hard-core" marathon runner. There are also many great stories surrounding Boston, such as the time in 1984 when Rosie Ruiz was declared the winner of the women's race – only for officials to later discover that she had covered most of the race via subway!

Another marathon legend centers around Bill Rodgers, a hometown boy who was known as "Boston Billy." Rodgers won the race four times, including the 1975 race where he stopped to tie his shoelace and still won by a wide margin!

Dozens of wheelchair, hand-cycle, and disabled racers traditionally lead off the Boston Marathon.

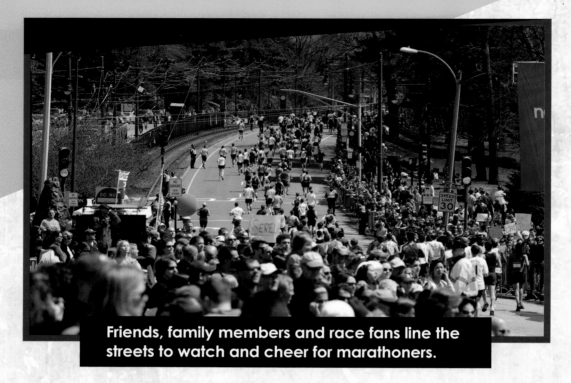

Friends, family members and race fans line the streets to watch and cheer for marathoners.

The race is also important to the local community. Every year, about one million people come out to watch the race and cheer for the runners. Tradition has it that the Boston Red Sox baseball team plays a home game every Marathon Day, and spectators come from Fenway Park to urge on the marathoners.

The course also winds its way through Wellesley, home of the famous all-women's college, where so many students come out to yell encouragement that this section of the course is known as the "scream tunnel." Some sections of the course are lined with musical bands and well-wishers handing water and other refreshments to runners. Others prefer to support the athletes on the toughest part of the course, as they climb the famous **"Heartbreak Hill"** late in the race, and the largest throngs gather at the race's finish on Boylston Street.

The race also receives media attention all around the world, with television crews coming from many countries outside the United States, and running fans closely following the times of the top male and female runners. As well, many runners travel to the race from around the world with their friends and families, adding a personal touch to the huge crowd of spectators.

All in all, with so many runners and fans taking part, the Boston Marathon has a true place in American sporting history as a classic event for both spectators and athletes.

The Wheelchair Race

Today, most major marathon races feature a wheelchair division. But Boston was one of the first. In 1975, a wheelchair athlete named Bob Hall made a bet with the race director of the time, Will Cloney: If Hall could finish the race in under three hours, Cloney would have to recognize him as an official finisher, and give him a BAA Certificate in recognition of his efforts. Hall completed the course in 2:58 — and Cloney made good on his promise, thus opening up the Boston Marathon to wheelchair racers. Today, the course record is an amazing 1:18:25 by Josh Cassidy of Canada!

Fans, racers, and officials filled the street at the finish line of the 2013 Boston Marathon about an hour before the bombing.

Chapter 2
The Fateful Race

The runners who lined up to start the 117th edition of the Boston Marathon on April 15, 2013, looked forward to a great day of running. The weather was a little cool for spectators, at about 47 degrees F (8 °C) at the start of the race, but ideal for the runners. There were more than 23,000 competitors, from all fifty U.S. states plus the District of Columbia, as well as ninety-two countries, ready to go at just after 9:15 AM, when they paused for 26 seconds to honor the twenty-six people who were tragically killed at Sandy Hook Elementary School in Newtown, Connecticut, a few months earlier.

The first wave of participants to leave the starting line in Hopkinton was the wheelchair athletes, followed by the Elite women's division, and then the Elite men. The rest of the marathoners left the start in three waves over the next forty minutes.

Throughout the course and at the finish line, fans saw some exciting action. Hiroyuki Yamamoto of Japan won the men's wheelchair race in a time of 1:25:33, while Tatyana McFadden of the United States took the women's wheel-chair crown in 1:45:25.

In the Elite men's race, Ethiopian Lelisa Desisa beat Kenyan Micah Kogo and countryman Gebre Gebremariam in an exciting sprint finish. Desisa won in 2:10:22, just five seconds in front of Kogo, who was in turn just one second ahead of Gebremariam! Desisa won $150,000 for first place.

In the women's event, Rita Jeptoo of Kenya had a much wider margin for the win, her time of 2:26:25 putting her thirty-three seconds in front of Meseret Hailu of Ethiopia, who was three seconds ahead of Sharon Cherop of Kenya, the 2012 winner. Jeptoo took home a $150,000 first prize.

Smooth Start

Race day in 2013 seemed pretty typical of most Boston Marathons, and for the first few hours after the initial competitors left the starting line, everything was as it had been in previous editions of the race. In fact, race officials had conducted two standard sweeps for bombs in the area near the finish line, and found no evidence of any danger. As had been the case in previous years, spectators and finishers were allowed to enter and leave the finishing area as they pleased. With so many runners and so much of their gear in backpacks and athletic bags, along with discarded water bottles and the general chaos of officials, fans, and race finishers, the Boston finish line is always a pretty chaotic place. But all in all, there was nothing to suggest that the 2013 edition of the Boston Marathon would be different than other years.

Survivor Account

As a player for the New England Revolution pro soccer team, goalkeeper Matt Reis was used to saving soccer balls fired at him. But at the finish line of the 2013 marathon race, he also became a life-saver. Reis was waiting with his young son, Jacob, ready to cheer on his wife, Nicole. But when Reis heard the first bomb blast, he knew something was wrong – and that was confirmed when he saw his father-in-law, John Odom, lying in a pool of blood. **Shrapnel** from the first bomb had ripped into the older man's legs, and he was in very serious condition. Reis acted quickly, and saved Odom's life by tying his jacket and belt around the leg wounds in an effort to stop the bleeding. In fact, Odom lost so much blood his heart stopped beating twice – but he did survive and, after being on life support for 10 days and undergoing 11 operations, started to learn to walk again.

For his part, Reis, who is retired from playing and is now a coach for the Los Angeles Galaxy team, says he wasn't acting heroically – he was just doing what he had to do.

"For me the biggest thing was just trying to think positively, not think of the worst, and try to mentally make sure that he pulled through it," said Reis. "Something like this where your life really truly flashes before your eyes, you realize what's important to you."

Smoke billowed as a bomb exploded into the stunned crowd on April 15, 2013, at the Boston Marathon.

Chapter 3

2:49 PM: the Moment of Horror

Almost exactly two hours after men's race winner crossed the finish line, however, the 2013 Boston Marathon became anything but a normal race.

At 2:49 PM, with almost 6,000 runners still on the course, the area near the finish line on Boylston Street was rocked by two explosions, about 200 yards (183 m) and thirteen seconds apart. Because of the noise from the bombs, spectators several blocks away wondered later if some kind of special finishing cannon was being fired off to welcome runners in to the race's end. Initially, in the confusion that followed the explosions, spectators, runners, and race officials were unclear as to what was happening, and some runners continued to cross the finish line for about eight more minutes.

Soon, though, those on the scene realized that windows on nearby buildings had been blown out by the force of the bombs. Far worse, though, was the human damage that soon became apparent: The two bomb blasts killed three spectators, and injured 264 more – seventeen of whom were taken to hospital in critical condition.

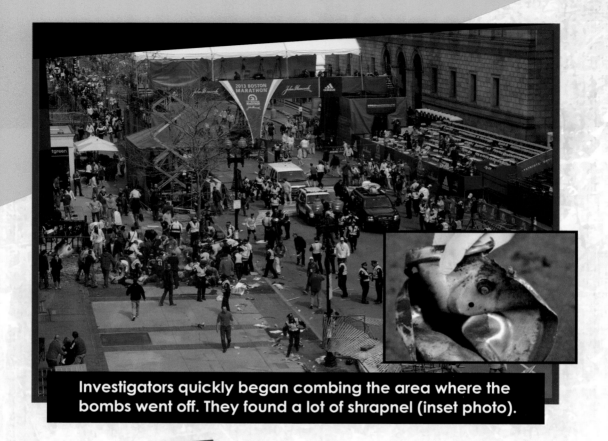

Investigators quickly began combing the area where the bombs went off. They found a lot of shrapnel (inset photo).

The Bombs

The bombs had been hidden in two backpacks that had been left in the huge crowd of race fans at the finishing area. The explosions quickly changed the 2013 Boston Marathon from a tradition annual celebration to a horrible disaster.

The bombs had contained shrapnel – material that flies off in all directions when exploded – including nails, ball bearings, and sharp metal, which cut into legs, arms, and other body parts of people who were hit, resulting in many serious injuries. Emergency personnel treated victims for serious cuts, loss of blood, and severely damaged limbs. In the days that followed, at least fourteen people had to have arms or legs **amputated**.

When investigators examined the scene, they discovered that the bombs were what is known as **pressure-cooker bombs** – explosive devices that can be made at home using a regular kitchen pressure cooker, shrapnel, and a timing device. A pressure-cooker lid was found on a rooftop near the explosions, as well as the remains of an electronic circuit board and some pieces of nylon from a backpack.

Non-Finishers

Because of the bombings, more than 5,000 runners and wheelchair athletes could not complete the race. Many had come oh-so-close to the finish, and all had trained hard for a very long time to be able to compete – only to have their dreams wiped away by this terrible act.

Race organizers from the BAA gave special medals to all those runners who could not complete the race that day. As well, they increased the number of participant spots available in the 2014 race for those whose 2013 event came to an unfortunate end.

Initial Reponse

Police, emergency medical services, and other first responders reached the scene immediately. A standard post-race medical tent that had been set up to help race finishers was quickly turned into a place where those injured by the bombs could get help.

Police moved quickly to stop the race, and diverted runners to safer locations away from the official finish line. Using an emergency plan that was in place before the race, they evacuated buildings and locked down the area within fifteen blocks of the blasts. The Massachusetts Army National Guard also assisted police and emergency medical workers in helping people who were injured – and many spectators did whatever they could to assist people who had been hurt.

Because of the threat of other bombs going off, police bomb squad members had to inspect all the backpacks and

The City of Boston had good plans in place that allowed first responders to arrive quickly

runners' bags that were left lying around the area. Luckily, no other explosives were found.

As safety precautions, ground traffic at Boston's Logan International Airport was halted, and public transport such as subways and buses was stopped. But as the chaos subsided and the injured were taken to get treatment, the difficult task of finding out who was responsible for the bombing attack began.

Survivor Account

Dr. Natalie Stavas won't soon forget the events of April 15, 2013. And neither will many survivors of the bombings who were lucky she was nearby when the explosions hit.

Dr. Stavas completed the marathon on a broken foot she'd fractured in training. But, much more importantly, when her race ended, she went from marathoner to life-saver.

As the 32-year-old neared the finish line, running alongside her dad, Joe – also a doctor – she heard the bomb blasts and immediately started helping anyone she could find. Victims required mouth-to-mouth oxygen, tourniquets, and wounds to be closed, and Dr. Stavas and her dad worked quickly to aid those who had been hurt.

What's more, she donated the $6,000 she had raised for charity by running the race to the Boston Medical Center's pediatric emergency department after the race.

"As a physician, " Dr. Stavas told reporters after the race, "I take an oath to do the best I can." Luckily for many survivors of the bomb attacks, her best involved saving lives.

As the smoke from the bombs rose, some people in the crowd watched in shock while others hugged and cried.

Chapter 4

Broken Dreams

For many marathoners, being able to compete at Boston is a dream come true. They train for hundreds – if not thousands – of hours and miles to run in this prestigious race, and most have to meet qualifying standards just to earn the right to be on the starting line. For most of the participants, even with no chance of winning the race, competing in Boston is a chance to improve on their own personal best time.

Many people from all over the world arrange to meet friends at the race, perhaps to run together, or to cheer one another on. Others run in support of a charity or other good cause, collecting pledges and donations. Fans also show up for a chance to see some of the world's best long-distance runners in action – and some just line the course because they want to cheer on the participants as a way of being part of the race.

For thousands of people, these dreams exploded when the two bombs detonated at the marathon finishing area. Millions more watched in shock as the events in Boston were broadcast worldwide.

Casualties

Three people lost their lives in the bombings of April 15, 2013. All of them were spectators who had come out to cheer on the runners, never suspecting that the day might end in tragedy.

One of them, Krystle Campbell, was a 29-year-old from nearby, Arlington, Massachusetts, who worked as a restaurant manager. Friends and family remembered her as a woman with a "heart of gold" and "happy, outgoing" person who had been attending the race as a spectator since she was little. "Oh, she was a beautiful girl," her grandmother, Lillian Campbell, told the media. "She was just beautiful. She was a fun-loving girl."

Another casualty was eight-year-old Martin Richard. He was from Dorchester, Massachusetts, and was watching the race with his mother and sister, who were also seriously hurt in the bombing. His family and neighbors recalled that Martin was a big fan of the Boston Red Sox, and the city's hockey team, the Bruins – and was also a skilled athlete in his own right who also took the time to help classmates who struggled with their homework.

The name of the third person killed in the Boston Marathon bombings was initially not released to the media after the bombings. The only information available about

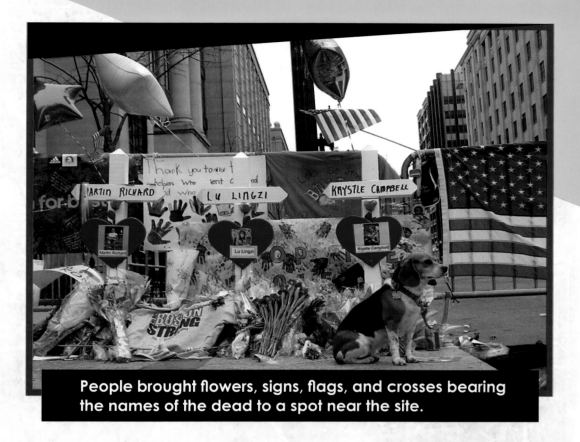

People brought flowers, signs, flags, and crosses bearing the names of the dead to a spot near the site.

this person at first was that she was a graduate student in mathematics at Boston University who had been watching the race with friends – some of whom were also hurt.

The student's family asked that her name not be released, and officials and the media respected that request. Soon, though, it was revealed that the student was Lu Lingzi, a 23-year-old from Northern China. In cooperation with Lu's family, Boston University set up a scholarship in her name. "She's gone," Lu's father said at her memorial service in Boston. "But our memories of her are very much alive."

Injuries

Doctors, nurses and other health care workers treated the 264 people hurt by the bombs at almost thirty hospitals in and around Boston.

One victim, a 34-year-old Massachusetts roofer named Marc Fucarile, stayed in the hospital for 100 days after the attack, until his release in July 2013. Doctors had to amputate his right leg above the knee, and treat him for broken bones in his leg and foot. Like many people hurt by the explosions, Fucarile also had **perforated eardrums** from the noise of the bombs, as well as serious burns and shrapnel wounds.

Fucarile had been near the marathon's finish line to watch a friend at the end of the race. Two other friends, who had also been spectators, lost their lower right legs as well. Doctors who treated the victims said these lower-leg injuries were common because the bombs had been placed low to the ground.

Two other spectators, brothers J.P. and Paul Norden, had come to watch a friend in the race. From nearby Stoneham, Massachusetts, the brothers, who were 33 and 31 on the day of the explosions, each lost a leg in the explosions, and went through fifty operations between them. Both spent

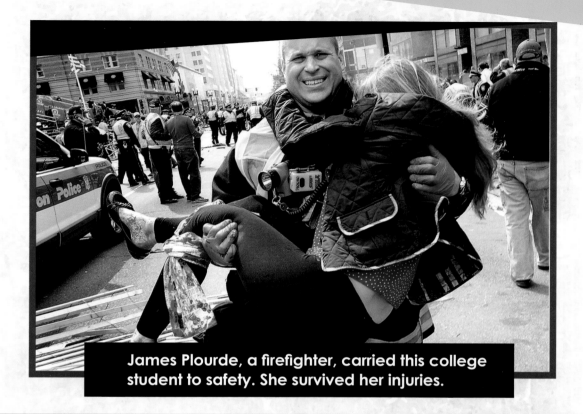

James Plourde, a firefighter, carried this college student to safety. She survived her injuries.

Survivor Account

The Boston Marathon bombings could not stop professional dancer Adrianne Haslet-Davis from returning to the stage. In March 2014, she performed a short routine at a conference in Vancouver, British Columbia, Canada – with the help of a specially designed bionic prosthetic leg designed for her by Hugh Herr, a scientist from the Massachusetts Institute of Technology and a double amputee himself.

Haslet-Davis was injured in the attack along with her husband, US Air Force Major Adam Davis. "I was always determined to dance again," she told reporters. "I knew that I had to, that I would, and here I am."

Emergency crews rushed 118 people to hospitals. The first one arrived just nine minutes after the bombing.

a lot of time in the hospital and now walk on prosthetic legs. J.P.'s fiancée, Jacqui Webb, was also hurt in the attack.

While it took a long time for both brothers to recover, they were both helped a lot by the One Fund Boston charity. Each received $1.2 million from One Fund Boston to help with medical expenses and to move ahead with their lives. "I don't know what my life will bring," J.P. said one year after the bombings. "I don't know how work will be; I don't know what type of job I will be capable of working."

Survivor Account

Of all the stories of survivors from the 2013 attacks, perhaps none is as touching of the one involving James Costello and Krista D'Agostino.

Costello, who made an annual tradition of going to watch the race, was badly hurt in the attack, suffering shrapnel wounds and very severe burns that required several skin grafts. A well-known photograph was published in newspapers and online that showed him staggering away from the site of the explosion in badly torn clothes.

But during his treatment and recovery, he met D'Agostino, a nurse. Over time, the two fell in love and married in August 2014.

"I'm actually glad I got blown up," Costello joked on the Today television show. "I wish everyone else didn't have to, but I don't think I would ever have met her if I didn't, so I'm pretty happy."

Heroic Bystanders

In any kind of disaster, professionals such as police, firefighters, doctors, and other medical personnel are trained to spring into action to help people who have been hurt and to prevent further injury and even death. Usually, these first responders follow a pre-set plan for dealing with crises, arriving on the scene quickly and acting effectively and efficiently.

A race official helped a 79-year-old runner stunned by the blast as a police officer (left) drew her gun. The runner was not seriously injured.

But in the face of a disaster, it is also the so-called everyday people at the scene who find themselves acting heroically to help people. Often these people have only very basic training in helping accident victims – but find it within themselves to do things such as closing up wounds, performing CPR, or pulling people away from the accident scene to get help from more experienced medical workers.

At Boston, the famous spirit of togetherness was very much in action when the two bombs went off. Many everyday heroes saved lives of people hurt by the blasts simply by thinking and acting quickly.

Women at Boston

Today, men and women run the Boston Marathon in more or less equal numbers. But it wasn't always that way. For the first seventy years of the race, Boston was a men-only race.

In 1967, five years before women were allowed to compete officially, a runner named Kathrine Switzer made a big breakthrough in this regard. She entered the race as only "K.V. Switzer" and was moving along quite comfortably until the race director, Jock Semple, attempted to remove her from the race by knocking her to the ground. Semple did not succeed, though, as Switzer's running partner (and boyfriend), a burly fellow named Tom Miller, sent Semple tumbling to the ground with a shove. The photos of that mid-race tussle gained so much attention around the world that soon, races everywhere would allow women runners!

Their actions are even more remarkable when you consider that they could not be sure that there were not other bombs about to go off – meaning they were helping others despite the fact that they may have been hurt themselves.

One person who acted fast to save others was a race volunteer named Devin Wang, then a student at Boston University and a champion synchronized skater. "I think instinct kicked in, knowing that there were spectators in that general area, not knowing if there's going to be another explosion, not knowing what I was going to see once I got there," she said later. "I felt like I did not do as much as so many other people, yet I was getting all the credit for being that hero."

Survivor Account

Many people who saw the shocking news footage of the aftermath of the Boston Marathon bombings will remember Carlos Arredondo as "the man in the cowboy hat" who pushed an injured spectator to safety in a wheelchair. What people only learned later was that Arredondo's heroism was just the latest story in a life marred by tragedy, but colored with hope.

Arredondo, who was born in Costa Rica, lost a son in the Iraq war in 2004. Another son committed suicide in 2011 battling depression. Arredondo and his wife Melida have worked hard to raise awareness of suicide, especially as it relates to service in the military.

Carlos Arredondo (center) pushed badly injured Jeff Bauman to medical care with help from Paul Mitchell (left) and Devin Wang.

At the 2013 Boston race, Arredondo was watching near the finish line, cheering on members of the a suicide support group and the National Guard, when the bombs hit. He immediately began helping to clear away barricades that had toppled onto people as a result of the blasts, and assisting people who were hurt. He is captured in an unforgettable photo, pushing a survivor named Jeff Bauman in a wheelchair to receive medical attention. Bauman had both his legs blown off by the bombs and was losing so much blood he would have certainly not survived if not for the quick thinking and heroism of Carlos Arredondo.

President Barack Obama thanked the medical responders when he visited wounded survivors of the bombing at Massachusetts General Hospital on April 18, 2013.

Chapter 5

Boston Fights Back

The world struggled to understand why these attacks had happened, and who had been responsible. U.S. President Barack Obama condemned the bombings. "We will find out who did this," he told reporters at the White House. "We'll find out why they did this. Any responsible individuals, any responsible groups, will feel the full weight of justice."

Immediately, investigators began asking the public for help in finding out who was behind the attacks. Photos or video taken by spectators can often be very helpful in these situations, and so can closed-circuit camera footage from the scene. Indeed, on April 18, the The Federal Bureau of Investigation (FBI) released pictures and video of two suspects – one who was captured on photo putting something down where the second bomb went off.

The FBI took over the search for two men who had been identified on video as possible suspects. The pair were identified as Dzhokhar Tsarnaev, who was 19 at the time of the bombing, and his brother, Tamerlan Tsarnaev, who was 26. The brothers were from Chechen backgrounds, meaning their ancestors came from a region located to the southeast of Russia.

A short time after the FBI released pictures of the brothers, they went on the run, allegedly killing a police officer at the Massachusetts Institute of Technology, and carjacking a Mercedes SUV with the help of a gun. The SUV driver and hostage later reported that one of the men told him he was one of the Boston Marathon bombers. The hostage was forced to take money from a bank machine to give to the gunmen, who are reported to have talked about escaping to New York City.

When the brothers stopped at a gas station, the SUV driver managed to get away. He called police and told them that because he had left his mobile phone in the vehicle, they could track it remotely. Just after midnight, police in the town of Watertown, just outside Boston, saw the brothers and tried to arrest them. This led to a dangerous gun battle, with the brothers tossing explosives at police while gunfire was exchanged. Fortunately no civilians were hurt in the fight as they had been warned by the police to stay off the street.

One police officer, Richard Donohue, was badly hurt by the gunshots, but survived. As the battle reached its conclusion, police tackled Tamerlan, but Dzhokhar drove off in the SUV, running over his brother as he sped away. Dzhokar soon abandoned the vehicle and took off running. Tamerlan had been shot several times in the gun battle with police. He died at a nearby hospital as doctors were unable to save his life.

Boston Shutdown

Soon, police had embarked on a door-to-door manhunt in and around Watertown and surrounding area. Police and the FBI closed off a large section of Watertown and warned everyone to stay indoors and off the streets. They also warned residents just how dangerous the man they were looking for was. On April 20, a resident noticed blood stains around a boat he had parked in his backyard. Taking a closer look, he found the seriously injured Dzhokhar. The man called police who apprehended and arrested Dzhokhar immediately. On April 22, federal officials charged him with the use of a weapon of mass destruction in the Boston Marathon attacks. Police also noted that, if Dzhokhar were to be convicted, he could face the death penalty.

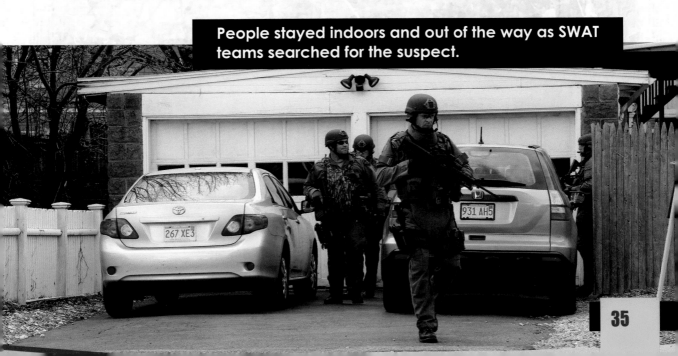

People stayed indoors and out of the way as SWAT teams searched for the suspect.

In the months that followed, Dzhokhar was charged with more than thirty crimes surrounding the Boston Marathon attacks, but he pleaded not guilty to all of them. His trial began in Boston in November 2014. At the time this book was being written, the trial of Dzhokhar Tsarnaev had divided many people in Massachusetts over the issue of the death penalty. In one 2013 survey, about one-third of Boston citizens said they favored this form of punishment for Dzhokhar, while more than half said they would rather see him receive a sentence of life in prison without parole. Dzhokhar was charged under federal laws, which means he could face the death penalty even though Massachusetts has abolished it. No prisoner has been put to death in the state since the 1950s.

An image from a security camera shows the Tsarnaev brothers (Dzhokhar in the back) carrying backpacks just before the bombing. This helped police and witnesses identify them.

Survivor Account

Jarrod Clowery is a carpenter and professional pool player who was hurt in the bombings. Two friends who were standing nearby lost legs, and during his time in the hospital recovering from serious leg wounds, he became discouraged that he would ever get well again, often finding himself in tears.

It wasn't until he began getting letters from schoolchildren wishing him and other survivors a successful recovery that he began to believe he could get better.

"I was reading the letters and, instead of crying and being scared, I was laughing," he said. "I was still crying but now they were tears of joy. I started to see the best of humanity, not the worst."

But it still took Clowery a while to feel mentally ready to face the world again. Over time, he did, starting the Hero's Hearts Foundation that recognizes everyday heroes and works to prevent bullying in schools. He also has spent time ice fishing with his friends who were hurt in the attack.

"For a period of time, [it was like] the bomb never went off," he said. "We were just friends again. Things are going to be normal. It's just going to be a different kind of normal."

The Perpetrators

Following the death of one of the bombers and the arrest of the other, people tried to figure out why the Tsarnaev brothers had carried out their bombing attacks on the Boston Marathon. Another big question was whether or not they had any ties to formal terrorist organizations. U.S. President Barack Obama summed it up well in a speech when he wondered aloud: "Why did young men who grew up and studied here, as part of our communities and our country, resort to such violence?"

Soon, the media began to put forward a picture of the two men. Dzhokhar had come to the United States with his parents in 2002. His older brother, Tamerlan, joined them a year later. Before immigrating to the United States, the Tsarnaev family had lived in Kyrgyzstan and the Russian republic of Dagestan.

Many people were surprised to hear that Tamerlan had also been a successful amateur boxer. In 2009, however, it became clear that he had embraced several of the teachings of radical Islamic **clerics**. The FBI had been advised by the Russian government in 2011 to look into his possible terrorist activities, but found no evidence. In 2012, though, he visited Dagestan for six months – and when he came back to the United States, he created a YouTube channel, linking to some videos about terrorism. It was in that same year that he applied for U.S. citizenship.

Investigators learned that Dzhokhar was a well-liked student at the University of Massachusetts, Dartmouth. In fact, three of his school friends discovered a backpack containing fireworks with the powder taken out of them in his dormitory room. Because these three students threw away the backpack (which investigators later found) they were arrested and charged with obstructing the investigation into the Tsarnaevs. One of the trio, Azamat Tazhayakov, was found guilty in July 2014, and faced a maximum sentence of twenty-five years in prison.

London Marathon Support

Just five days after the Boston Marathon bombing, participants in one of the world's largest marathons pledged to help the survivors and show their support for the victims. The 36,000 runners in the London Marathon observed a thirty-second period of silence before starting the race, and many ran with black ribbons pinned to their shirts. A huge crowd of 700,000 spectators cheered on the runners in London, and many of them also wore black ribbons.

London race director Hugh Brasher said the world's running community had been "shocked and saddened" by the events in Boston. Brasher added that a very careful security check of the race took place before the start – and that everyone concerned with the London race had decided that "the show must go on." The 2013 London Marathon was completed without any incidents.

Several temporary memorials grew around the bombing site. The items were collected by the city after several weeks and preserved for future display.

Chapter 6
Honoring the Survivors

Of course, the capture of the two men responsible for the bombings could not reverse the terrible toll that the attacks had taken – in terms of the deaths and injuries that took place, but also the fear and sadness they caused. But the people of Boston, and their supporters around the world, soon rallied to help the stricken city.

Leaders around the world denounced the attacks, and offered condolences to the families of the victims. Organizers of other races also decided to express their support for Boston. For example, the officials at the Vancouver Sun Run, a 10 km (6-mile) race which is the largest 10 km run in the world with upwards of 60,000 participants, decided to donate $10 from every late race entry. Other runners banded together for a cross-country relay from Los Angeles to Boston in June, 2013 to raise money. The relay included more than 2,000 runners covering 5 to 12 miles (8 to 19 km) each, over fourteen states. Many other races observed moments of silence before their starts, with runners wearing special shirts or ribbons to honor the victims and their families. Most observers agreed that the marathon community around the world came together like never before to commemorate Boston.

Boston Strong!

The post-bombing support for families and survivors came together under the slogan "Boston Strong." The slogan was made popular on Twitter and soon spread quickly, appearing on T-shirts, bumper stickers, and posters. Many famous people expressed their support for the city while wearing Boston Strong shirts, although others began to suggest that, after a while, it had become over-used and over-commercialized.

One of the greatest expressions of the Boston Strong slogan occurred in the fall of 2013, during the Boston Red Sox baseball team's celebrations after winning the World Series. Two Sox players, Jonny Gomes and Jarrod Saltalamacchia, walked to the Marathon finish line and placed their trophy there.

One Fund Boston

As Boston recovered from the bombings, Mayor Thomas Menino observed that the collection of money set up to help victims and their families, known as One Fund Boston, was truly something special. "In my twenty years as mayor," Menino said, "I've never seen the business community come together so quickly."

In honor of One Fund Boston, the city's Prudential Tower was lit at night with a giant number 1. As well, almost 25,000 people pledged more than $2 million online,

One Fund Boston, the charity created to help the marathon victims, collected more than 200,000 donations from more than 60 countries.

and a special Boston Strong concert took place at the city's well-known TD Garden arena, with musical artists of all kinds performing to raise money for One Fund.

One Fund Boston had raised almost $70 million in support of victims of the bombing, and their families. Many people used the funds they received to pay for medical and rehabilitation expenses. Others, whose injuries made it impossible to work as they recovered, were able to cover basic living expenses with what they received.

The Future of the Boston Marathon

The Boston Marathon shows no signs of stopping or even slowing down despite the bombings in 2013. Runners from around the world will always see the race as a classic challenge to strive for, and the people of Boston and surrounding towns will continue to crowd the streets to support the runners.

One runner, John Farah, summed up why he and many other runners intended to run Boston the year after the attacks – and why they planned to keep doing so. "I'm running it to make a simple statement: Acts of cowardice will not stop me from exercising my rights as an athlete and a human," said Farah, "I am running it for those who were injured and can't run it. I am running it for the love of running. I am running it to show my support for all Bostonians."

Increased Security

For the 2014 race organizers took extra security measures. Almost 4,000 police officers in uniform were there on the day, and backpacks, suitcases, strollers, and glass containers were forbidden at the race site. As well, bag checks and extra security barriers were in place. But it was also important for police to maintain the positive, friendly feeling that has always surrounded Marathon Day. The 2014 race went off without any incident.

Boston was determined to show the world that the marathon would go on in 2014.

Glossary

amputate Surgically removing a limb that has become infected or unable to be used by a patient.

Boston Athletic Association (BAA) The group that organizes the Boston Marathon

cleric A member of the clergy, or a priest, in any religion.

eardrum a membrane of the middle ear that vibrates in response to sound waves.

Heartbreak Hill A major incline about six miles from the finish of the Boston Marathon; considered by many to be the toughest part of the race course.

marathon A 26 mile, 385 yard (42.2 km) running race

Patriots' Day A holiday celebrated in the states of Massachusetts and Maine, commemorating early battles of the Revolutionary War. Today it is observed on the third Monday of every April.

perforate To make a hole or a series of holes in (something).

Pheidippides According to Greek legend, the soldier who ran from the Battle of Marathon to Athens, announcing the Greek victory over the Persians and becoming the first ever marathon runner.

pressure-cooker bomb An explosive device made from a common kitchen pressure-cooker filled with explosive material.

prosthetic A word to describe a human-made device that replaces a missing body part.

shrapnel Material such as metal or other metallic objects, that explodes out of a bomb and causes injury.

For More Information

Books

Bauman, Jeff. *Stronger.*
New York, NY: Grand Central Publishing, 2014.

Bruschi, Tedy, Fultz, Jack. *If Not for the Perfect Stranger: Heartwarming and Healing Stories of Kindness from the 2013 Boston Marathon.*
Chicago, IL: Bantry Bay Publishing, 2014.

Derderian, Tom. *The Boston Marathon: A Celebration of the World's Premier Race.*
Chicago, IL: Triumph Books, 2014.

Petersen, Justin. *Boston Marathon (World's Greatest Sporting Events).*
La Jolla, Ca: Scobre Educational, 2015.

Websites

Because of the changing nature of Internet links, Rosen Publishing has developed an online list of websites related to the subject of this book. This site is updated regularly. Please use this link to access this list:

http://www.rosenlinks.com/SD/Boston

Index